Dadabhai Naoroji
Britain's First Asian M.P.

Written by
Zerbanoo Gifford

Illustrated by
Petra Röhr-Rouendaal

MANTRA

Foreword

10 DOWNING STREET
LONDON SW1A 2AA

THE PRIME MINISTER

It is now a hundred years since Dadabhai Naoroji was elected as the first non-white member of the House of Commons. Since then the contribution made by members of the ethnic minorities to British life has been rich and varied – in business, in the arts, in sport and, I am glad to say, increasingly in the world of politics.

I want all our people to feel part of the community in which they live. It is my aim to build a country of choice and opportunity where individuals can get to the top of their chosen field because of what they have done, not because of where they have come from – and no matter what their colour or their religion.

Dadabhai Naoroji showed a hundred years ago what people of talent can achieve. I hope and believe that in the years ahead more and more members of our ethnic minorities can follow his shining example

John Major

May, 1992

HOUSE OF COMMONS

LONDON SW1A 0AA

The Office of the
Leader of the Opposition

May 1992

Dadabhai Naoroji came to Britain in the mid-1850's to pursue
a career in business, but his great energy, his strong sense
of justice and the breadth of his interests rapidly drew him
into campaigning for progressive political causes in Britain
and India. His active contribution to the public life of both
countries continued for fifty years.

In celebrating the centenary of his election to Parliament we
honour his memory and his historic achievement. And we
applaud those who have followed in his wake — from India and
many other countries — who, often in the face of opposition
and prejudice, have enriched the commercial, cultural and
political life of Britain.

Neil Kinnock

Neil Kinnock

Foreword

The Rt Hon Paddy Ashdown MP

HOUSE OF COMMONS
LONDON SW1A 0AA

This book serves as a timely reminder of the contribution
made to British politics by an extraordinary individual.
Dadabhai Naoroji, first Asian Member of Parliament in
Britain, social campaigner and founder of Indian nationalism,
was indeed a truly remarkable man. His demand for far
reaching social and educational reform, both in India and in
Britain, established him as a progressive Liberal, and earned
him the respect of many of his contemporaries, including the
Leader of the Liberal Party, William Gladstone. He was a
pioneer who led the way forward for others to follow. This
book is a fitting tribute to the achievements of a great man.
It will, I hope, help to bring about a greater understanding
of his contribution to British political life.

Contents

For Lal and Shobhna Chellaram – for sharing Dadabhai's devotion to education

A Note on Language.
In this book, "Indian" means anyone whose family comes from the Indian subcontinent, now divided into the countries of India, Pakistan, Bangladesh and Sri Lanka.
As we will see, in Naoroji's day, the area was divided differently and the British often referred to Indians as "natives" of the subcontinent of India. Naoroji too used this language in his writing and speeches.
Similarly, in his day, many people called Muslims "Mohammedans" as a reference to the prophet Mohammed.
In quotations from Naoroji and his contemporaries, such outdated terms have been retained for historical accuracy.

Picture Sources:
Hulton Deutsch Collection: Cover, 7, 27, 41 and 46
National Maritime Museum: 16
P & O: 16 The Publishers would like to thank P & O for their help
Zoroastrian Trust Funds of Europe: 42, 47

Mantra Publishing Ltd
5 Alexandra Grove
London N12 8NU

Typeset by Finepoint Graphics, London
Printed and Bound in Great Britain by BPCC Wheatons

Chapter 1
The Best Kept Secret

In 1892, Dadabhai Naoroji became the first Indian member of the British *House of Commons* when he won the London seat of Finsbury Central for the *Liberal Party.* Overcoming many difficulties, he had arrived at the political centre of the *British Empire.* Yet one hundred years later, many of his pioneering achievements have been forgotten in Britain, becoming perhaps the best kept secret of British political history.

Naoroji was a remarkable man. He dedicated his life to political, economic and social *reform* in both Britain and India. When in *Parliament,* he spoke about India, because he saw himself not only as the representative of the people of Finsbury, but also as the voice of India, then around 250 million people.

His refusal to compromise his basic beliefs won him respect from friends and opponents alike. An unwavering commitment to the need for Indians to play a role in the *government* of their own country led Naoroji to become known as the "Grand Old Man of India".

In many ways, Naoroji was more *radical* than most other politicians of his day. He championed causes such as equality for women and supported moves to improve working people's lives by reducing working hours and introducing pensions to ensure that the elderly were free from poverty when they retired. He saw the British *House of Lords* as unrepresentative of Britain's people and argued for its abolition. At a time when only the well-off could afford to be a Member of Parliament, he saw the need to pay *MPs* a salary to enable everyone, rich or poor, the chance to stand for the House of Commons.

Some of the problems of Naoroji's time remain with us today. Britain still suffers from *racial discrimination,* the under-representation of women and minorities in Parliament and the *economic exploitation* of poorer countries by the richer.

Yet Dadabhai Naoroji had the courage to realise that there are causes that are worth fighting for even when the road to success is difficult. When faced with *racial prejudice* from other politicians and the press, he did not give up, but became more determined to win justice for everyone affected by such ignorance.

Such strength of character and selfless devotion to justice should not be forgotten.

Britain in India

At the time of Naoroji's birth, most of the Indian subcontinent was run by the British East India Company, a private firm which was granted a *charter* by Queen Elizabeth I on 31st December 1600 to have a *monopoly of trade* in the East Indies – Asia.

The original aim of the Company was to capture the Indonesian spice trade from the Dutch. But after they defended their highly profitable monopoly with force, including killing some English traders, it was decided to concentrate on the larger Indian subcontinent where the main European competitors were the French.

The profits made by the East India Company were substantial. Its monopoly in Indian cotton goods, silks, spices and saltpetre (in great demand in Europe as an ingredient of gunpowder) enabled investors to make large sums of money for many years. Gradually, driven by the desire to make even more money, the company expanded its influence in India.

India was then a mix of many states. By the time Western traders arrived, most of the subcontinent was under the control of the Muslim Mogul emperors. With the death of the emperor, Aurangzeb in 1707, what central government there was, died with him and many areas asserted their own independence.

In the political chaos that followed, the European companies stepped in, fearing a loss of their profits, and slowly started taking over effective control of more and more Indian territories. At the same time, the British East India Company, helped by the Royal Navy, gradually pushed out its French rivals in a series of wars mirroring conflicts in Europe.

The increasingly powerful East India Company was reorganised and given the right to coin its own money, have power over British subjects in its own areas, raise its own armies in India and even make war against non-Christian countries. In effect, it was a private nation.

The position in India was reviewed by the British Parliament every twenty years. Gradually, the company's powers were taken away and given to Government bodies. In 1858 the East India Company was abolished and India came under the direct rule of the British crown.

India was now officially part of the British Empire. So anyone, like Naoroji, who wished to change things in India, had to deal with the British political system with its heart in London.

Chapter 2
Humble Origins, High Achievements

Dadabhai Naoroji was born on 4th September 1825, in the fishing village of Mandvi, near Bombay, India. His father was a poor Parsi Zoroastrian priest, Naoroji Palanji Dordi.

When Dadabhai was four, his father died leaving Dadabhai's mother, Manekbai, to bring him up alone. To raise a child on one's own takes much hard work and self-sacrifice which Naoroji recognised when he wrote about his mother many years later:

Widowed when I, her only child, was an infant, she voluntarily remained a widow, wrapped up in me, her everything in the world. She worked for her child, helped by a brother. Although illiterate [she was] a wise woman. She was the wise counsellor of the neighbourhood. She helped me with all her heart in my work for female education and other social reforms against prejudices of the day. She made me what I am.

At one point, it was expected that Naoroji would follow in his father's footsteps and become a Zoroastrian priest himself. His religion was certainly very important to him and formed the basis of his character and values throughout his life.

Arranging marriages between children was customary in those days and at the age of eleven Naoroji was engaged to a seven year old girl, Gulbai. They were duly married when they were adults but sadly it was not always a happy marriage as they had different personalities. Gulbai showed little interest in Naoroji's political and social campaigns.

It was even suggested that Naoroji divorce Gulbai but he refused. However, wanting to prevent others from being obliged to marry partners picked for them when they were young, he vigorously campaigned against the practice of arranging marriages between children. Later Mahatma Gandhi, another famous Indian, also felt he had been married too young and supported ending this custom.

Naoroji had a very successful academic career. With the help of a scholarship he studied at Bombay's famous Elphinstone College. Mountstuart Elphinstone, after whom the college was named, had been the British Governor of Bombay. Deeply committed to education, he founded the Native Education Society despite the beliefs of many that the "natives" did not need the benefits of schooling. After Elphinstone's retirement in 1827 the grateful people of Bombay raised money to start a new college in his honour.

The young Naoroji continued to excel at his studies and in 1846 the Chief Justice of Bombay, Sir Erskine Perry, offered to pay half the cost of sending him to England to study as a *barrister*, on condition that the Parsi Zoroastrian community paid the other half.

Being educated in Britain was seen at the time as a necessary step for any Indian who wished to progress in life. But Sir Erskine Perry's offer was declined as the Parsi community remembered the conversion by missionaries of two Parsi boys in Bombay and they were worried that the same might happen to Naoroji if he went to Britain.

So Naoroji stayed in India where he decided to become a teacher instead of a lawyer. At a time when the top academic posts in India were all held by the British, he soon became an Assistant Professor of Mathematics in Bombay and then went on to become the first Indian Professor. Looking back on his life, Naoroji said that this first was one of his proudest achievements in a lifetime filled with "firsts".

In addition to pursuing his academic work, Naoroji started a newspaper, *Rast Gofter* ("Truth Teller") to help promote female education and many other social reforms. One of his campaigns concerned the status of widows. In those days many Indian people considered widows to be unlucky and to be avoided. Naoroji, whose own mother had been widowed early in her life, wanted to remove the stigma attached to widowhood and to enable them to remarry and take a full part in community life if they wished.

While Indian boys found it difficult to receive a good education, girls were considered not to need any academic education at all. Naoroji disagreed and helped start classes for girls in friend's homes in Bombay, one of the first steps in starting permanent schools for Indian girls.

In 1855, Naoroji accepted an offer from the Cama family to enter into business with them in England. Their's was the first Indian firm to be established in Britain. However the partnership was short-lived and ended after just three years. One of the reasons was that Naoroji refused to become involved with the highly profitable trade in opium and thereby make money out of other people's misery. Once again, his social perspective was far in advance of most of his contemporaries, both British and Indian.

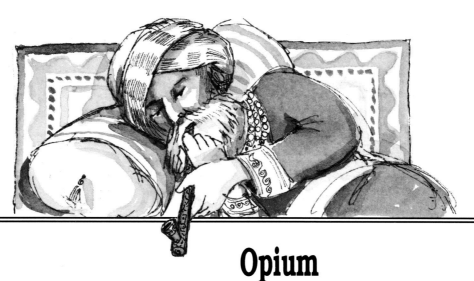

Opium

Opium is a drug that comes from the juice of the immature Oriental or Opium Poppy, grown in Asia and the Middle East. It has been used for thousands of years to relieve pain and to treat stomach problems. It's still used in medicine today.

Although highly addictive, opium is also taken for pleasure. The first British ambassador to India in 1615, was sent to the court of the Mogul emperor Jehangir, who was an opium user. Opium smoking spread to China from India soon afterwards.

The export of Indian opium to China quickly became an extremely profitable trade to the British. As the problem of addiction grew, the Chinese emperors objected and tried to stop opium coming in. To maintain their profits, the British fought two wars in the 19th century, known as the Opium Wars. British rule of Hong Kong is based on their victory in these two conflicts.

The British Government made a great deal of money out of the opium trade through taxation. It justified allowing the trade by saying that moderate use of opium had no ill effect. Missionaries who had seen the effects on people in China disagreed, as did Naoroji. He said that it was "a sin on England's head and a curse on India for her share in being the instrument."

It was only when opium became a problem in Britain too that the non-medical use was eventually made illegal.

But even today, the British Government still makes billions of pounds out of taxing a highly dangerous and addictive substance which kills around 100,000 people in Britain each year – tobacco.

During his first visit to Britain, Naoroji's successful academic career continued when he was appointed Professor of Gujarati at University College London, becoming the first Indian professor at a British university. He was later appointed a Life Governor of the College.

In 1857 while Naoroji was still in Britain the Indian Rising, known in Britain as The Indian Mutiny, broke out.

Lord Dalhousie, the Governor General of India, had sought to "westernise" the country. While some of his reforms were for the good, others deeply offended many people, and tensions between the British rulers and the ruled rose sharply.

The feelings of injustice came to a head in an incident involving the East India Company's army in India, which was mostly made up of Indian soldiers, *sepoys*, under British officers. A rumour started that new rifle cartridges were greased in beef and pig fat. Particularly as the ends of the bullets had to be bitten before they could be fired, this was extremely offensive to both Hindu soldiers (to whom the cow is a sacred animal) and Muslim soldiers (to whom eating pork is forbidden) and they refused to use the new bullets.

The Rising rapidly developed into a very bitter war affecting much of northern India. Both sides behaved brutally and in the end the Rising was harshly put down. News of the Rising was a great shock to the British government and it led directly to the end of the East India Company. Britain took over all responsibility for running India in August 1858.

On his return to India that year, Naoroji proposed that a statue be erected in Bombay to show the loyalty of its people to their new Queen. Given the legacy of bitterness many people had towards the British following the previous year's Rising, this would have been a controversial suggestion even though Bombay itself was not involved in the fighting.

But Naoroji must have felt that his faith in the British was justified when Queen Victoria promised that her new Indian subjects would be treated equally in an official *Proclamation* in 1858:

We hold ourselves bound to the Natives of our Indian territories by the same obligations of duty which bind us to all our other subjects; and those obligations, by the blessing of Almighty God, we shall faithfully and conscientiously fulfil...

And it is our further will that ... our subjects of whatever race or creed be freely and impartially admitted to offices in our service, the duties of which they may be qualified, by their education, ability and integrity, duly to discharge.

Naoroji soon returned to Britain, this time to start his own trading firm in Liverpool. He quickly became highly respected as an honest businessman and someone prepared to help friends in difficulties. Naoroji also continued to refuse to deal in opium, wine or spirits.

The Suez Canal
the New Link to India

Naoroji travelled to Britain from India and back many times during his life. Today, Air India advertisements tell us that 'India is just nine hours away'. It was not always so.

When Naoroji first came to England in 1855, he used a ship which sailed around the coast of Africa, past the Cape of Good Hope. The journey of approximately 20,000 km from Bombay to Southampton took about two months to complete.

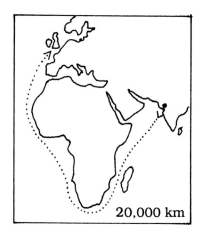

20,000 km

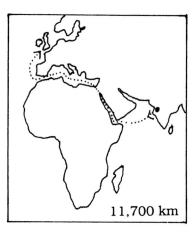

11,700 km

In 1869 the Suez Canal was opened. This 169 km waterway, at the point the continents of Africa and Asia meet, was one of the engineering triumphs of the 19th century.

Once the Suez Canal had opened, the sea journey between Bombay and Southampton was drastically reduced to just 11,700 km.

Combined with the effect of faster ships, it later took Naoroji less than a month to get from London to Bombay.

Interestingly, if you add up the length of all his voyages, you find he spent a total of over two years of his life on board ship, travelling between the two countries.

As well as his business activities, Naoroji once again occupied himself with a broad range of other interests. In 1861 he was a founder member of the London Zoroastrian Association, which remains a focal point for Zoroastrians living in Britain today.

Although the original reason for Naoroji coming to Britain was commerce, being at the heart of the British Empire meant it was easier to influence the people who ruled India from afar.

It is a sign of his greatness that Naoroji was always less interested in personal wealth and more concerned that India should receive fair treatment from the British.

Chapter 3
Good Thoughts, Good Words, Good Deeds

India is a multi-ethnic, multi-religious country with Hindus, Muslims, Sikhs, Jains, Buddhists, Jews, Christians, Zoroastrians and more. Naoroji was a Zoroastrian. Because Zoroastrianism is little known in Britain, it is interesting to discover its history and beliefs.

Over 3,500 years ago, a man called Zoroaster was born. *The Guinness Book of Records* lists him as the earliest named prophet and the religion he founded is called Zoroastrianism. Before then, all religions we know of believed in the existence of many gods but Zoroaster taught that there was only one, who he called Ahura Mazda. He also separated the sources of good and evil in the world, evil being the work of Ahriman.

Zoroastrians believe that people must always try to work for good, to make the world a better place. It is the duty of all human beings to have Good Thoughts, use Good Words and do Good Deeds. After death, the actions of each person will be judged. Depending on how they have lived on earth, souls either go to join Ahura Mazda in heaven or are sent to Ahriman's hell. These ideas have influenced many religions.

Persia was a Zoroastrian land from the time of Zoroaster, and there were many powerful and generous kings who, even when they conquered foreign lands, respected the defeated peoples' religions. Unlike most other religions, Zoroastrians do not try to convert others to their faith.

One famous Zoroastrian king was Cyrus the Great. In 538 BC he conquered Babylon, a city now in Iraq. Babylon was, in turn, the centre of a large empire which had captured people from many lands. Amongst those Cyrus freed to go home were the Jews who had been held in exile for many years. They were given help to return to Jerusalem and rebuild their temple there. Because of this, Cyrus is praised in the *Old Testament* as the "King of Kings".

No empire lasts for ever and, around 641 AD, Persia was conquered as part of the new Muslim expansion following the death of the prophet Mohammed.

The majority of Persians converted to Islam and life became hard for the remaining Zoroastrians.

Over a century later, many of the Zoroastrians decided to emigrate and they set sail from their Persian homeland, landing at Sanjan in 785 AD.

The story of what happened when they arrived at the small fishing village in Gujarat on the west coast of India is a very special one for Zoroastrians and Naoroji would have heard it as a young boy.

The story tells that the Zoroastrian *refugees* were taken in front of Raja Jadhva Rana, the local Hindu ruler. The king explained that his country was too crowded and there was no room for new settlers. To demonstrate this, he took a bowl and filled it with milk until it was so full that not one more drop could be added. But the Zoroastrian High Priest called for a little sugar. He carefully put it into the bowl, where it dissolved without spilling any of the milk. "Perhaps your land is full, but we will enrich it with our presence, without displacing any of your people or your customs."

This so impressed the king and his assembled subjects that he asked the Persians what they would need if they were allowed to settle. He was told that they required only the freedom to bring up their children according to their own traditions, the freedom of worship, and enough land to feed themselves. They did not want to be a burden on their new homeland.

The Gujarati ruler Raja Jadhva Rana had the foresight to allow the Zoroastrian refugees to stay in his land. He offered them a home, but he also made certain conditions which would benefit both communities, by making the new settlers less conspicuous. The first of these was that the women should wear the local costume, the sari.

The second condition was that they must learn Gujarati so that they would be able to take part in the life of their adopted country. Without knowing the local language they would have become isolated, second-class citizens, unable to communicate effectively. Nevertheless, they could, and did, retain their own language and customs as well.

Thirdly, the Raja asked them to explain their religion, which they had kept despite suffering so much, and for which they were willing to start a new life in a country so far away. The king's genuine interest in his new subjects meant each learnt from the other.

History has shown that the Zoroastrians were true to their word and did enrich the whole of India. In return, the Indian peoples welcomed them. Neither lost their culture and both benefited from each other's way of life.

The Zoroastrians became known as Parsis, people from Persia. By being given a sense of belonging in India, they contributed generously to the life of the community. There is an Indian phrase which sums this up, "Parsi, thy name is charity."

Although Naoroji was proud to be a Zoroastrian Parsi, he considered himself an Indian above all else. He once said,

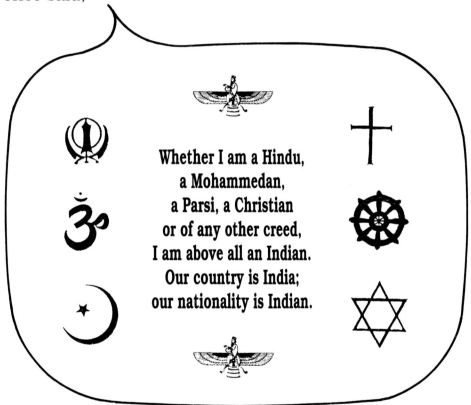

Whether I am a Hindu,
a Mohammedan,
a Parsi, a Christian
or of any other creed,
I am above all an Indian.
Our country is India;
our nationality is Indian.

He never forgot that when the Parsis needed a safe refuge, it was Indians who had granted it to them. The political message from this remained of great importance to him throughout his life — to be proud of one's country and try and serve it to the best of one's ability.

Chapter 4
Naoroji's Role in the Indian Independence Movement

While in London, Naoroji founded the East Indian Association in 1866 to help inform the British about the subcontinent, its people and their needs. Branches were also started in India, attracting the support of many Indians, from princes to businessmen.

Since there was no direct representation of Indian interests in Government, the Association acted like a modern *pressure group*, sending information to MPs, asking questions and trying to influence Government policy indirectly.

As part of the Association's work, Naoroji set out to discover the cost of British rule in India. It was clear that while Britain was getting richer, India was becoming poorer. But no-one, not even the Government, kept proper records of expenditure and income. The person officially responsible for Indian finances kept two completely different sets of records and did not know which was the more accurate.

It turned out that the Indian Administration was the most expensive in the world. India was asked to pay for much of Britain's army and navy, including many units not involved in India's defence. India, a much poorer nation than Britain, was made to pay higher taxes.

A huge programme of public works, including a massive railway network, had brought great benefits to India. However the cost, paid for by India, had been excessive partly due to a lack of proper planning.

As with today's developing countries, much of India's expenditure went on paying large amounts of interest on loans, and not on building up the country. Britain made sure that the value of the Indian currency, the Rupee, was kept artificially low so that it could buy

Indian exports cheaply. It also ensured that India exported raw materials such as cotton rather than finished goods which would compete with factories in Britain.

Naoroji also noted that "Europeans occupy almost all the higher places in every department of Government... While in India, they acquire India's money, experience and wisdom, and when they go, they carry all of it away with them. Thus India is left without those elders in wisdom and experience... who guide the destinies of their country... a sad sad loss."

Worse still was the discrimination that Indians faced in their own land. In all but a few organisations started by the British, Indians, he wrote, "however fit and desirous to join, are... deliberately and insultingly excluded. The Europeans are, and make themselves, strangers in every way."

The name Naoroji put to the effects of the removal of so much of India's wealth for Britain's benefit was "The Drain Theory". He went on to write a 700 page book, *Poverty and Un-British Rule in India*, to explain the theory and was also called to give evidence on the subject to Parliament.

Ironically, the things the British did in India – building the railway and communications systems, starting national newspapers – enabled the Indian independence movement to develop and grow. Although Queen Victoria's Proclamation on becoming Empress of India had promised fair treatment, this was not the reality experienced by the people in India. Feelings that they were being exploited and discriminated against grew.

The need for unity to improve the conditions in India led Indians active in politics to join together. In January 1885, the Bombay Presidency Association was formed as a political pressure group, with Naoroji as vice-president. Later that year, when a *General Election* was called in Britain, the Association sent three men to campaign for candidates who supported Indian interests and against those who did not.

At that election, a distinguished Indian from Bengal, Lal Mohun Ghose, stood for Parliament as the Liberal candidate for Deptford. He was the first Indian to contest a British Election, but was defeated, as unfortunately were most of the other candidates the Association supported. But involvement in British politics, and the need to have an effective voice for India in the House of Commons, started Naoroji thinking of becoming an MP himself.

In December 1885, Naoroji helped found the *Indian National Congress* in Bombay. Seventy-three delegates from across India came together to discuss their vision of India's future. Around half of the delegates were lawyers, the rest were journalists, businessmen, landowners and professors. They were the new educated Indian middle class, united in believing that the ideals of *democracy* and equality Britain taught had not been practised in India because the British put their own interests first.

Delegates saw Congress' first task as liberalising and reforming British rule in India. "Not one single genuine voice is there in Parliament to tell at least what the native view is on any question," Naoroji told Congress.

He became one of the strongest voices to be heard in Britain on behalf of India. He soon made friends with the British MPs interested in the subcontinent whom he asked to raise matters in Parliament on his behalf. He published dozens of pamphlets and spoke at many public meetings on the unacceptable effects of British rule in India.

Naoroji remained unselfish in the tireless work he did on behalf of his countrymen, and was deeply loved in return, becoming the most important politician in the "moderate phase" of the Indian National Congress. After he became an MP in 1892, large crowds would turn out to greet him whenever he returned to India. The only other Congress personality later to draw such vast numbers was Mahatma Gandhi.

Following in Dada's Footsteps

Dadabhai Naoroji and Mahatma Gandhi were good friends. In 1888, Gandhi came to Britain as a young man to study law. He later recounted how he met the "Grand Old Man of India", then in his sixties:

"One of my friends suggested that I should seek Naoroji's advice. Though I had brought a written introduction to him from India, it seemed to me that I had no right to trouble such a great man.

[I attended any meeting addressed by Naoroji and] at last mustered up the courage to present him with my letter of introduction. 'You can come and have my advice whenever you like,' he told me."

Gandhi discovered that Indian students in Britain had free access to Naoroji who became a father figure to them. Indeed, Gandhi used the word 'dada' (father) in talking about the relationship between the two. He also described visiting Naoroji's home and seeing the office in which Naoroji did so much of his work for India. It was a small room, just 2.6m by 2m, so full of paper that little space was left for a desk and a chair.

Later Naoroji became "a constant adviser and inspiration" to Gandhi in his fight for justice in South Africa. He wrote to Naoroji every week, receiving a personal handwritten reply each time. When the government of Natal (part of South Africa) proposed taking the right to vote away from people of Indian descent, Gandhi was preparing to leave the country.

Naoroji wrote that it was important to stay and fight this unjust measure and, with Naoroji's support from Britain, Gandhi gradually developed his techniques of non-violent resistance known as *satyagraha* ("steadfastness in truth") which he later used to such effect in helping gain Indian Independence.

Chapter 5
Mr Narrow Majority

On 13th April 1886 the Indian newspaper *The Hindu* announced that Naoroji was leaving for Britain to stand for Parliament at the next election. "As an authority on Indian economics," it added, "there is none equal in all India."

At that time, the two major political parties in Britain were the *Conservative Party* under Lord Salisbury and the *Liberal Party*, led by William Gladstone. The Conservatives sought to represent the interests of landowners and were largely opposed to changing the way the country was run. Indeed, when he was Conservative Prime Minister after his successful career as a general, the Duke of Wellington declared in 1830 that Britain's system of government was perfect.

The Liberals disagreed and when in government, passed a series of *Acts of Parliament* which ended many of the abuses of power, allowing many more men to vote and have their say in running the country. Votes for women were still many years away.

It was clear from their record of reform that someone like Naoroji would choose to join the Liberal Party. He sought advice and support from many British political figures and his meetings with almost all the leading names of the Liberal Party are to be found in his diary.

Just two weeks before the 1886 General Election, Naoroji was unanimously selected by the local Liberal party in Holborn, London, to be their candidate. In accepting the *nomination*, he dealt with the issue of representation for India in Parliament:

I appeal to you for the sake of the two hundred and fifty millions of India. I have a right to do so, because I know that India regards me — at least, so it is said — as a fair representative. I want to appeal to you in their name that, whether you send me or another to Parliament, you at once make up your minds that India ought to have some representation in your British Parliament.

One newspaper, on hearing of Naoroji's selection, wished him "pronounced" success, although his name was "difficult to pronounce". However the *constituency* had a long record of electing a Conservative MP and Naoroji did not have enough time to become well known in the area. That he would lose was never in much doubt, but his performance, gaining 1,950 votes compared with 3,651 votes for the Conservative, Colonel Duncan, was highly credible and he learnt much about fighting elections.

In those days the *electorate* was much smaller than it is now. Today, an average constituency has 60,000 to 80,000 voters and nearly everyone over the age of eighteen has the right to vote. A hundred years ago, the same area would have well under 10,000 voters. This was because, firstly, the population of Britain was less than half of what it is now.

Secondly, no women were allowed to vote (Naoroji's support of the new "Votes For Women" campaign was in contrast to most Victorian politicians). With some other disqualifications, that left most men over the age of twenty one, but not everyone registered their right to vote.

After the 1886 election, in which Lal Mohun Ghose had again stood and again lost, Naoroji began his search for a more winnable seat. By March 1887, he had decided to try for Finsbury Central, another London constituency. It had been won by a Conservative, Captain Penton, with a majority of just five votes and, not surprisingly, many other people wanted the Liberal nomination for this seat.

After several months sifting through names, the local Liberal selection committee short-listed four potential candidates, Naoroji among them. In August 1887, a vote among party members to select their candidate had the following result:

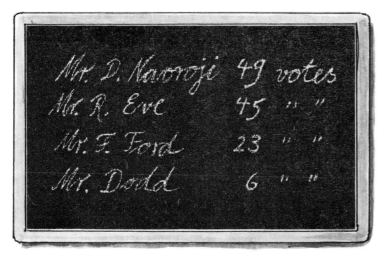

The secretary of the local Liberal Association, Mr Jacobs, and the other candidates all congratulated Naoroji on the result. He went home, sure that he would be the Liberal candidate. A letter was also sent from the national Liberal Party, approving his selection.

Next day, however, Mr Jacobs called for another meeting to vote again to decide who to nominate. It was said that the first vote had not been taken properly. Naoroji's refusal to accept this and to attend the new meeting, probably contributed to the result of the second vote, in which Mr Eve was victorious.

Thus started a long-drawn out dispute. Naoroji spent almost as much time trying to get his original nomination accepted as valid as he did in meeting voters in what he still expected would be his constituency. These arguments took three years to resolve and were only settled when Mr Eve decided to fight another constituency instead. By June 1890, Naoroji was once more confirmed as the candidate for Finsbury Central.

Meanwhile, he had become a national figure in Britain thanks to a speech in Edinburgh by the Conservative Prime Minister, Lord Salisbury. Naoroji's opponent in the 1886 Holborn election, Colonel Duncan, retired as an MP in 1888. As a result, a *by-election* was fought in the constituency to elect a replacement MP. Both parties picked new candidates for the by-election which the Conservatives won, but with a much reduced majority.

Lord Salisbury, who had been Secretary of State for India, gave the following excuse for his party's poor result:

> *It was undoubtedly a smaller majority than Colonel Duncan obtained [back in 1886], but Colonel Duncan was opposed by a blackman, [Dadabhai Naoroji]. However far we have advanced in overcoming prejudice, I doubt if we have yet got to that point of view where a British constituency would elect a blackman.*

This speech outraged nearly everyone except the audience that night, who greeted it with cheers. Queen Victoria was dismayed and reprimanded her Prime Minister. The National Liberal Club held a special banquet to show its support of Naoroji. When the details of the speech spread around the world, Naoroji even received a letter from Australia saying that Lord Salisbury was wrong.

Another Indian in London at that time was Muhammad Ali Jinnah, later to become the first Prime Minister of Pakistan. "If Dadabhai was black, I was blacker," Jinnah wrote to his sister. "And if this was the mentality of the British politicians, then we would never get a fair deal from them." Indeed, Lord Salisbury's "blackman" speech unwittingly convinced many people of the need for Indians to be represented when decisions affecting their country were made.

Back in the constituency of Finsbury Central, Naoroji enjoyed six months in which his candidature was uncontested. However in January 1891 another of the original four contenders, Mr Ford, announced that he would be standing as the Liberal Candidate, supported by several members of a new local Liberal Association. Local newspapers were divided, *The Holborn Guardian* supporting Ford, while *The Weekly News and Chronicle* supported Naoroji.

This new dispute became even more confused than the first. The national party organisation was split between people who thought Ford should be the candidate, people who thought Naoroji should be chosen and people who wished the whole mess would go away and that they should do nothing to help either side. Although Naoroji had the support of most of the leading figures in the national party, nothing positive was done to help him, much to his and his supporters' annoyance.

These problems had sapped much of Naoroji's financial resources. When news of his troubles reached India, the press there had no doubt that racial prejudice was at the heart of the matter, and that Naoroji should give up his electoral ambitions and return home. But he refused to give up.

His father's old family name, Dordi, means "a rope made of coir". Naoroji once said, "You may burn a dordi, but you can never take the twist out of it. So it is with me. When I form a decision, nothing will dislodge me from it."

Rather than give up the candidature he felt was rightly his, Naoroji was prepared to have two "Liberal" candidates contest Finsbury Central even if it meant losing the seat to a Conservative. He risked being very unpopular with the national party, but in the end he was successful. After a year spent disputing the nomination, Mr Ford finally withdrew.

At the next General Election, held on 6th July 1892, Dadabhai Naoroji was the sole Liberal candidate for Finsbury Central. Among the people who actively supported his campaign were both Mr Eve and Mr Ford, who wished to prove that their earlier opposition to him was neither personal nor racial.

In fact, Naoroji received the whole-hearted support of many well-known figures of the time. Florence Nightingale, who supported the cause of Indian freedom, wrote encouraging letters from her sick bed. Josephine Butler, the social reformer and a leader of the campaign to allow women to vote, lent her support for his "uncompromising friendship of womanhood" and for his long record of upholding the necessity of equal laws for men and women.

One of the founders of the *trade union movement*, Keir Hardie, helped Naoroji get the support of working class voters. Mr Hardie was standing as a candidate for the *Independent Labour Party* in another constituency at the same 1892 election and carved a place in history by becoming the first MP for what is now the *Labour Party*.

Mahatma Gandhi and Muhammad Ali Jinnah both assisted in the election campaign. Jinnah was also to work as Naoroji's secretary and helped write some of his speeches. Mancherjee Bhownagree, an Indian barrister based in London, also *campaigned* for Naoroji, an experience he put to good use when he became the second Indian MP in 1895.

Although politicians regard elections as highly important, not all voters share their view! On election day, candidates need to have a group of people to remind potential supporters to vote. Particularly in *"marginal"* seats like Naoroji's, every vote is crucial.To help encourage people to vote, lifts to the polling station

are often offered to supporters. The Conservatives had many horse-drawn carriages supplied for this purpose by English aristocrats and Naoroji was grateful for similar support from Indian Royalty, especially the Maharaja of Baroda who lent twenty of his carriages from his London homes.

Once all the votes cast were counted, Naoroji had just three votes more than the Conservative candidate, Captain Penton, with 2,959 votes to 2,956. As the result was so close, Captain Penton demanded the votes were counted again in case any mistakes had been made. It must have been a very tense affair when a few errors were found, but fortunately the final result was that Naoroji's majority increased to five votes and he was declared the winner. Partly because many people found it difficult to pronounce his name, his constituents soon nicknamed their new MP "Mr Narrow Majority".

The news of Naoroji's victory soon reached India where it was received ecstatically. The Cama family, who had first enabled Naoroji to come to Britain, immediately sent one hundred guineas to the Lord Mayor of London's charity for the poor. (A guinea was one pound, one shilling, £1.05 in today's money). The message accompanying this considerable sum explained that the Zoroastrian religion encouraged people to share their joy with the less fortunate. On hearing of the gift, one newspaper wrote, "There are some things amongst the Parsis that we should do well to follow."

Not all papers were so positive. Two used the existence of a sacred fire that burns continuously in Zoroastrian temples to call Naoroji a 'fire-worshipper'. The Spectator complained, "If the electors of Central Finsbury like to be represented by a fire-worshipping Asiatic that is their affair and at all events shows absence of prejudice." Such absence of prejudice was surely needed in The Spectator and The St Stephen's Review which went even further: "Central Finsbury should be ashamed of itself at having publicly confessed that there was not... an Englishman, a Scotsman, a Welshman, or an Irishman as worthy of their votes as this fire-worshipper from Bombay." Just when Naoroji thought he had finally won a seat in Parliament, the defeated Captain Penton, accused some of Naoroji's helpers of "corrupt practices".

This is a serious charge in any election, and if found guilty, Naoroji could have been disqualified from becoming an MP. At best, there was a chance that Central Finsbury would have to re-run the election.

It turned out that the problem arose from the same carriages lent by the Maharaja of Baroda which had been so helpful on polling day. After some voters had been given lifts, they had also been given money for a drink by his helpers. Providing such refreshment for voters is known as "treating" and had been made illegal in 1883 to stop candidates bribing voters.

The case came to court in mid-December, after Naoroji had taken his seat in Parliament. However Captain Penton withdrew his complaint after two and a half days of the trial and both sides agreed to share the costs of the case.

Even at the age of sixty-seven Naoroji was a very active parliamentarian in what was to be Gladstone's last government. Naoroji was present for 90% of the *divisions* in the House of Commons. When constituents came to him with problems, he would try to ensure that the matter was put right. He spoke to many groups within Finsbury about the work he was doing on their behalf.

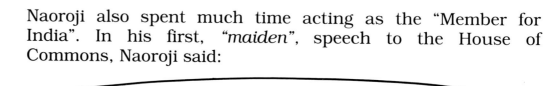

Naoroji also spent much time acting as the "Member for India". In his first, *"maiden"*, speech to the House of Commons, Naoroji said:

My election for an English constituency is a unique event. For the first time during more than a century of settled British rule, an Indian is admitted into this House as a Member...

He praised the decision to govern India on the lines of British freedom and justice, before going on to say that the result was that "a great movement of political life was infused" into India. He ended with these words:

So long as India is satisfied with the justice and honour of Britain, so long will her Indian Empire last. I have not the least doubt that, though our progress may be slow and we may at times meet with disappointments, if we persevere, whatever justice we ask in reason we shall get...

I hope that the connection between England and India — which forms five-sixths of the British Empire — may continue with benefit to both countries.

During his years in the House of Commons, Naoroji often spoke frankly and forcefully on matters relating to India. He repeated his belief in the "Drain Theory", saying that if Britain took less wealth and expertise out of India, both countries would benefit. One of his longest running campaigns was to get more Indians admitted into the Indian Civil Service.

Civil Servants

Civil Servants run the country. Guided by political leaders, they actually carry out the policies decided in Parliament and elsewhere. There are large numbers of *administrators* in any modern nation and it is important that they be representative, particularly as they decide many of the "small" details that are so important to everyone. The majority of letters written to MPs or councillors come as a result of dissatisfaction with the way people have been treated by these officials.

Dating back to the days of monarchs appointing their advisers, Britain's top civil servants came from the aristocracy. All this changed after the *Trevelyan–Northcote Report* of 1854 which recommended the creation of the Civil Service Commission. It introduced promotion on merit, based on difficult examinations.

Perhaps due to the backgrounds of the examiners, the exams were based on the *Classics* and *Humanities*. Young people who had not been to an English private school which concentrated on these subjects had little or no chance of doing well.

One of the reforms the British carried out in India during their rule was to introduce a similar civil service structure. Unfortunately, largely as the result of prejudice, all the officials of the Indian Civil Service were Europeans.

One of Naoroji's great campaigns was to have Indians admitted to the top levels of the civil service that ran their own country. Even when, under pressure, the policy of "no natives" was dropped, other obstacles were found.

The exams for the Indian Civil Service were only held in Britain. This meant that very few Indians could even compete because of the expense of travelling. The first hopeful Indian to try, a young Parsi called Rustamji Wadia arrived in London around 1860. Aged 22, he was told that he was a year too young to sit for the exam. Some later applicants were told they were too old. Frustrated and annoyed, Naoroji complained to the Secretary of State for India and tried to get the matter raised in Parliament.

Thanks largely to Naoroji's efforts, the position of Indian applicants improved. Eventually, the Governor General picked nine Indians annually to join the sixty people accepted for entry into the Indian Civil Service each year. Later still, exams were held in both India and England, so that Indians did not have to make the arduous and expensive journey to England.

In 1894, William Gladstone resigned as Leader of the Liberal Party having failed to keep his party united over the issue of *Home Rule for Ireland*. A year later Lord Roseberry, his successor as Liberal Prime Minister, called a General Election.

With such a "narrow majority" of just five votes, it was going to be difficult for Naoroji to retain his seat. A national swing of opinion against the Liberals meant that, despite a vigorous campaign, he lost his seat in the 1895 General Election by 2,783 votes to 3,588.

Chapter 6
Out of Parliament

Though Naoroji was now out of Parliament, he was certainly not out of politics. While an MP, he had used his influence to have a *Royal Commission* set up to investigate the state of India's finances. He now not only served as the only Indian member of the Commission, but also insisted on giving evidence to it. The Commission lasted four years and led to some improvements, although not as many as Naoroji and others had hoped.

To increase awareness of India's unhappy political and economic condition, Naoroji targeted a campaign in Lancashire, the destination of much of India's cotton exports. If India were wealthier, he argued, she could afford to buy more British goods and both countries would benefit from the lifting of the artificial restrictions on trade.

In 1900, the worst Indian famine for twenty-five years led to another campaign for Naoroji. He told his audiences that he was not just looking for famine relief, but for the future prevention of famine. He felt strongly that this could only be possible when money was invested in Indian agriculture and not used up in unfair loan repayments.

What industries there were in India were mostly owned by British investors, so the profits left India. Naoroji encouraged a Parsi family, the Tatas, to start the Tata Iron and Steel Works with Indian backing. The business prospered and today is still one of India's most important group of companies, covering all areas of the Indian economy.

Much to his disappointment, a serious illness meant that Naoroji was unable to contest the 1900 General Election. Afterwards, he resumed his search for a route back into Parliament. Alas, he ran into many of the same problems he had earlier faced in gaining the nomination for Finsbury Central.

After another disputed selections procedure in the London seat of Lambeth North, Naoroji eventually contested his last British election in 1906 as a Trades and Labour candidate.

It was a hopeless task. On polling day both Mr Myer (Liberal) with 2,162 votes and Major Gestrell (Conservative) with 1,904 votes out-polled Naoroji's 733 votes.

Sir Mancherjee Bhownagree
The Second Indian MP

Shapurji Saklatvala
The Third Indian MP

The 1906 General Election also saw the defeat of the second Indian MP, **Sir Mancherjee Bhownagree**, who had helped Naoroji win Finsbury Central in 1892. Bhownagree himself was elected as the Conservative MP for Bethnal Green, East London, in 1895. He was described by the Conservative party as a "True British Citizen". In contrast, many Indians were critical of his failure to oppose British Government policies towards India and nicknamed him "Mr Bow and Agree". Even so, Bhownagree joined with Naoroji in supporting Gandhi's fight to stop political rights being taken away from Indians in South Africa. He was also one of the organisers and benefactors of the Commonwealth Institute in London, opened in 1893, with the Bhownagree Gallery named after his only sister. Bhownagree was knighted in 1897 at the suggestion of the same Conservative Prime Minister, Lord Salisbury, who had earlier made the infamous "blackman" speech. Bhownagree increased his majority in the 1900 General Election, but lost his seat as part of a national swing against his party in 1906.

A founder of the Communist Party of Great Britain, **Shapurji Saklatvala** was the third Indian to be elected to the House of Commons. He first won his seat, Battersea North, London, standing as a Labour candidate in 1922, only to lose it the following year. Saklatvala was soon back in Parliament as a Communist after the General Election of 1924, having left the Labour Party over the issue of Indian independence.

At that time the only Communist MP in the House of Commons, he joked that his was the only party which always spoke unanimously. Nicknamed "Comrade Saks", his fiery views got him into trouble on several occasions and at one point he was imprisoned for two months after a speech in Hyde Park. At the 1929 election, Saklatvala was opposed by a Labour candidate and was defeated. It would be fifty-eight years before any other "non-white" MP sat in the House of Commons.

For most of his political life, Naoroji sought to explain to the British people the conditions of Indians and urge that they should be treated fairly. His aim was to improve the conditions of the "British Raj". However, in later years, he became disillusioned. At the International Socialist Congress in Amsterdam in 1904, he finally argued for *swaraj* or self rule for India. In his speech he said:

The Imperialism of civilisation is the Imperialism of equal rights, equal duties, and equal freedoms. The remedy is in the hands of the British people. They must compel their Government to fulfil the promises that they have made to India. The remedy is to give India self-government.

In 1906, the Indian National Congress was 21 years old and divided on a matter of policy. Some, mainly younger, delegates wanted to use force to remove the British from India. Others wished to use peaceful means, such as boycotting British goods. There were also those who believed that independence was not necessary and that British rule could be reformed.

The person most respected by all sides in this dispute was Naoroji and so he was asked to be the president of the 22nd Congress. Held in Calcutta, its meetings were attended by around 1,500 delegates, then the largest political gathering ever seen in India. In his speech, Naoroji repeated his call for swaraj but insisted that only peaceful methods should be used to end British rule in India. He also quoted the British Liberal Prime Minister, Sir

Henry Campbell-Bannerman, "Good government could never be a substitute for government by the people themselves."

After returning to Britain, Naoroji was seriously ill with bronchitis. He recovered by 1907 and left to live permanently in India where he was advised that the climate would be better for his health. In 1914, in an article on his life there, the British magazine *The Graphic* reminded readers that:

The great simplicity and purity of his life have been recognised and admired by all those who have come into contact with him...

During the past seven years he has lived in quiet retirement at a seaside suburb some fifteen miles from Bombay, enjoying the warm affection of his countrymen ...and the esteem of the heads of the Indian Administration.

When the King [George V] and Queen went out to India...they exchanged greetings with the distinguished veteran and [Naoroji] was visited by the new Governor of Bombay, Lord Willingdon, at the retreat where the evening light so gently falls upon him.

However Naoroji was not yet fully retired from political life. When the First World War broke out in August 1914, he declared that India should fight as part of the British Empire. In fact, one of his grandsons, Kershap, joined the British Army and was wounded fighting in France. Later, when Britain relaxed a ban on Indians being promoted to officer rank, Kershap was one of the first to be *commissioned* as an officer in the British Army.

On 30th June 1917, Naoroji died peacefully in Bombay. At his funeral, the Indian politician Sir Narayenraa Chandavarkar paid the following tribute to Naoroji's long life:

In his career, in all he did, in all he suffered, and in all he taught, he was the prophet Zoroaster's religion personified. Because he was the man more than anyone else of pure thought, pure words and pure deeds...

The sun that rose just ninety-two years ago over India has set. But I say that it is set to rise again in the form of a regenerated India, for Dadabhai Naoroji lived and worked for us with a devotion which must remain for all of us an inspiring example.

Chapter 7
A Dream Fulfilled

By the end of the First World War in 1918, over one million Indian soldiers had served in the Middle East and in France. Casualties numbered 121,598, including 56,423 men dead or missing. Just as the work British women had done during the war was partly responsible for women being given the vote soon afterwards, it was recognised that a sacrifice of this level by the people of India could not pass without giving India a small element of *self-rule*.

An official *Declaration* to this effect was duly made on 20th August 1917, less than two months after Naoroji's death. However, the promises were not fulfilled and British rule in India became increasingly unpopular. Many people lost faith in British justice when troops under General Dyer in Amritsar opened fire on Indian civilians who had been peacefully demonstrating against continuing restrictions on political activity, killing 379 and wounding 1,200.

During the 1920's, support for the independence movements grew – with Gandhi's tactics of non-violent struggle, everyone could take some part in the campaign, even if it was simply by not buying British goods.

Following much hardship endured by the people of India, full Indian Independence was finally won in August 1947.

If Dadabhai Naoroji, Member of Parliament, academic, businessman and social reformer, were alive today, he would be happy to see his main dream fulfilled — the countries of the Indian subcontinent are now independent and free to decide their own destinies.

Other campaigns he championed, such as education and equal opportunities for women and the ethnic minorities are now more advanced than in his own time, and that too, would please the "Grand Old Man of India". In his life, Naoroji encouraged Mahatma Gandhi to fight against the racist measures that led to apartheid in South Africa. Today, that inhumane system is starting to end. But he would remain saddened by the continuing levels of racial discrimination that are still to be found in societies across the world.

A true *internationalist*, Naoroji had a deep understanding of the benefits of the diversity that a multi-cultural society brings. One lesson he stressed was that immigrants can make an enormous contribution to their new country, if they receive the same welcome as the Zoroastrians had from India so many years ago.

Dadabhai Naoroji was undoubtedly one of the great men of his age, committed to equality and justice for all.

He believed passionately in the British sense of fair play, and he was convinced that if the British people thought a cause was just, they would support it. In a speech he had said:

I have observed that the English public as a body are very ignorant, and even to some extent misled, on Indian matters; but that whenever any subject is fairly and fully put before them, their decision is certain to be on the side of fair play, justice and honour.

Dadabhai Naoroji was a great believer in democracy, and his values remain as important today as they were in his own time. Rather than lead a violent *revolution*, he realised that the best way to change things for good was by persuasion and through the power of the ballot box.

"Persevere we must until the end" Dadabhai Naoroji 1825 – 1917

Glossary

Acts of Parliament: Laws agreed by both Houses of Parliament.

Administrators: People who carry out laws and decisions made by government.

Barrister: A lawyer trained to argue a case in court.

By-election: The election to replace an MP who has resigned or died.

British Empire: The area of the world outside the British Isles ruled by Britain. At its height, 1/4 of the world's people lived in the Empire, which covered 1/5 of the earth.

Charter: A formal document from the sovereign setting out rights and aims of a company or organisation.

Classics: The study of the languages of Latin & Ancient Greek.

Commissioned Officer: An officer in the British Army in receipt of papers confirming their rank.

Conservative Party: The political party which at the time of Naoroji sought to represent the interests of the well-off.

Constituency: The area represented in the House of Commons by an MP.

Democracy: Where most or all of the population takes some part in running a country usually by voting for people to represent their views. From the Greek words for 'people' and 'rule'.

Division: A vote in Parliament to decide an issue.

Declaration: An announcement.

Economic Exploitation: Where a country/company uses its wealth to take advantage of a poorer trading partner.

Election: Using a system of voting to decide an issue or choose someone.

Electorate: The people allowed to vote in an election.

Government: Making the decisions affecting a country or the people who do so. In Britain the government is made up of a section of the people in Parliament.

General Election: When an election is held in all constituencies in the country to elect an MP. Depending on the number of MPs elected, one or more political parties will form a new government.

Home Rule for Ireland: The desire for an independent Ireland after an Act of Union in 1800 made Britain and Ireland officially one country, ruled from London.

House of Commons: The elected Chamber of the British Parliament, now much more important than the House of Lords.

House of Lords: The unelected chamber of the British Parliament, its members include Britain's aristocracy.

Humanities: Subjects other than the sciences, ie modern languages, geography, history.

Independent Labour Party: Formed in 1898 it developed into the modern Labour Party.

Indian National Congress: An annual meeting of Indian politicians and people interested in India's future. It later became the main organisation fighting for India's independence.

Imperialism: Ruling one country from another.

Internationalist: One who believes that countries should work together.

Labour Party: The political party formed by the trade union movement in 1900. Originally named the Labour Representation Committee, it adopted its modern name in 1906.

Liberal Party: The political party which during Naoroji's time was the other major political party. Now known as the Liberal Democrats.

Maiden Speech: The first speech an MP makes in the House of Commons.

Marginal Seat: A constituency where more than one party is likely to win an election. Only about 1/3 of constituencies are marginal.

MP: Short for Member of Parliament. Someone elected to the House of Commons.

Monopoly of Trade: When only one company sells something. Companies with monopolies can make a great deal of money, because it knows customers have to pay high prices or go without.

Nomination: Without the backing of a political party candidates for Parliament are unlikely to be elected. The person supported by a party in an election is said to have that party's nomination.

Parliament: The group of people who make laws for a country. The Parliament of the UK consists of the Queen, the House of Lords and the House of Commons.

Pressure group: People who try to influence government by running campaigns.

Proclamation: An announcement.

Persia: An ancient empire. At its height it covered most of the Middle East, including modern Iran, Turkey, Iraq and Syria, extending as far as Egypt and NW India.

Radical: Someone who wants to see major changes.

Racial Discrimination: Judging people by their race, rather than on their abilities or character.

Racial Prejudice: The false belief that some races are better than others.

Reforms: Changes, hopefully for the better.

Refugees: People who have to leave an area to escape a disaster or persecution.

Revolution: The violent overthrow of a government.

Royal Commission: An important committee set up by Parliament to look into a specified subject and propose reforms.

Satyagraha: A campaign involving peacefully breaking unjust laws. When carried out by millions of people, as in India before Independence, it is impossible to arrest everyone, so the campaign encourages reforms.

Self-Rule: Allowing a country to run itself and make its own decisions. The opposite of imperialism.

Sepoys: Indian soldiers in armies run by the British.

Swaraj: A Hindi word for self-rule.

Trade Union Movement: The organisation of workers into unions, to give more power when bargaining with employers.